A Crocodile Finds His Missing Peace

John Strelkoff

Illustrations by
Childbook Illustrations

"Love the animals. God has given them the rudiments of thought and joy untroubled."

— Fyodor Dostoyevsky,
The Brothers Karamazov

ISBN-13: 978-1978233164
ISBN-10: 1978233167

Illustrations by Childbook Illustrations
Childbook Illustrations is the most loved children book
illustrations and publishing agency. With over hundred
titles illustrated, designed and published, the agency
is helping many authors fulfill their dream of getting
self published with ease and affordable pricing.
www.childbookillustrations.com

Dedicated to
Svetlana and Macarius

There was a young
Crocodile who lived
in a pond all alone.
He wanted so much to
make a friend but everyone
was afraid of him.

The other animals
would run away from him
because they were told,
"crocodiles are mean and dangerous!"
This made the young Crocodile sad.

One day, Father Ambrose
came to the pond to bless
the waters for Theophany.

The young Crocodile felt the love Father
Ambrose and the parishioners gave
to him and so he began to love God.

The young Crocodile prayed for
those who ran away from him.
He prayed for the birds, hedgehogs,
squirrels and other animals. He asked
God for their love and forgiveness.

Father Ambrose also prayed that
the young Crocodile would trust God.

When Crocodile finished school he loved God so much he wanted to help others find their way to Him.

From then on, Mr. Crocodile
would go with Father Ambrose
to bless the pond on Theophany.
They prayed that all the
animals would be safe.

The animals were no longer
afraid of Mr. Crocodile. He taught
them about God and His love.

With God's mercy, there was great peace
and love for every creature in the forest.

Mr. Crocodile was loved to the end of his days.
He passed away and was buried beside the
Church. Many of the animals still visit him today.

The End

Made in the USA
Middletown, DE
07 November 2020